MARK ZUCKERBERG

MEDIA ENHANCED BOOKS

AV2 BY WEIGL™

ADDED VALUE • AUDIO VISUAL

www.av2books.com

AV² provides enriched content that supplements and complements this book. Weigl's AV² books strive to create inspired learning and engage young minds in a total learning experience.

Your AV² Media Enhanced books come alive with...

Audio
Listen to sections of the book read aloud.

Key Words
Study vocabulary, and complete a matching word activity.

Video
Watch informative video clips.

Quizzes
Test your knowledge.

Go to www.av2books.com, and enter this book's unique code.

BOOK CODE

N338786

Embedded Weblinks
Gain additional information for research.

Slide Show
View images and captions, and prepare a presentation.

AV² **by Weigl** brings you media enhanced books that support active learning.

Try This!
Complete activities and hands-on experiments.

... and much, much more!

Published by AV² by Weigl
350 5th Avenue, 59th Floor
New York, NY 10118
Websites: www.av2books.com www.weigl.com

Library of Congress Control Number: 2015930426

ISBN 978-1-4896-3352-1 (hardcover)
ISBN 978-1-4896-3353-8 (softcover)
ISBN 978-1-4896-3354-5 (single user eBook)
ISBN 978-1-4896-3355-2 (multi-user eBook)

Printed in the United States of America in Brainerd, Minnesota
1 2 3 4 5 6 7 8 9 0 19 18 17 16 15

032015
WEP022615

Project Coordinator: Katie Gillespie   Art Director: Terry Paulhus

CONTENTS

Mark Zuckerberg **3**

MARK ZUCKERBERG

Since he first started learning about computers, Mark Zuckerberg has looked for new challenges. When Zuckerberg graduated from high school, **software** companies were eager to offer him a job. Full of ambition, he instead chose to learn more about computers at university.

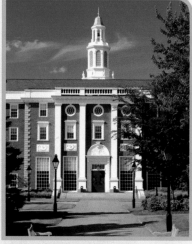

Zuckerberg studied psychology and computer science at Harvard University.

While studying at Harvard University, Zuckerberg started Facebook, a **social media** website. Only two weeks after its creation, half of the students at Harvard had joined Facebook. What began as a small project in Zuckerberg's dorm room has quickly become a multi-billion dollar company.

The story of Facebook's creation demonstrates the importance of education, creativity, and ambition. It also encourages young people to strive for excellence. Through his inspiring words, Mark Zuckerberg demonstrates how a combination of talent, luck, and hard work can lead to great success.

Mark Zuckerberg married pediatrician Priscilla Chan in 2012.

www.facebook.com/

Welcome to Facebook

facebook

ps you connect an
le in your life.

Mark Zuckerberg **5**

"The question I ask myself like almost every day is, **'Am I doing the most important thing I could be doing?'**"

"By giving people the power to share, **we're making the world more transparent**."

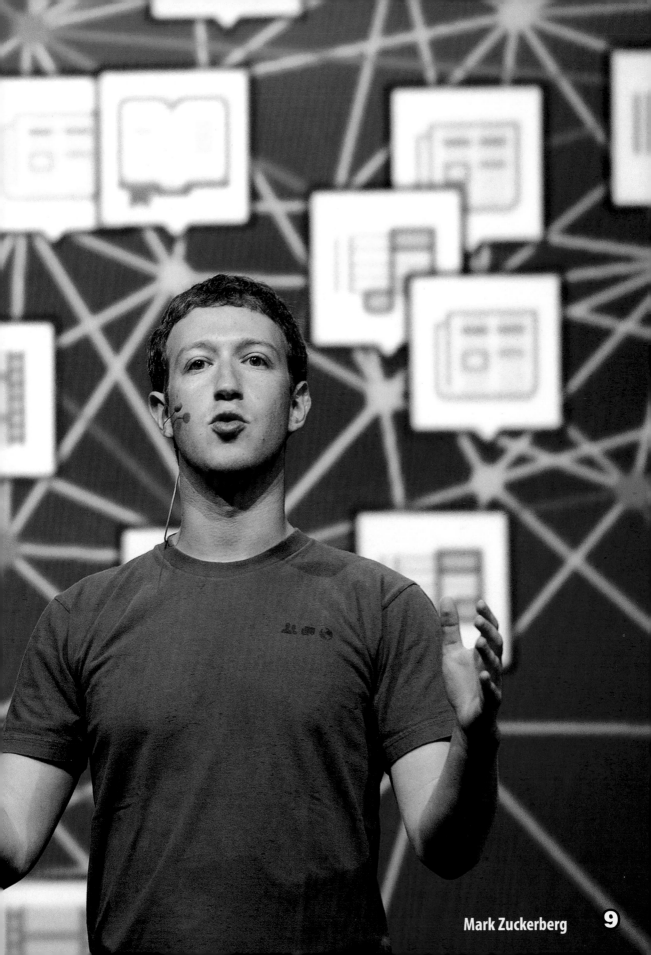

Mark Zuckerberg 9

"If you just work on stuff that you like and you're passionate about, you don't have to have a master plan with how things will play out."

Mark Zuckerberg 11

"The **biggest risk** is not taking any risk."

"[To] all of my friends who have **younger siblings** who are going to college or high school, my number one piece of advice is: **You should learn how to program.**"

Mark Zuckerberg

Quotes from the Greatest Entrepreneurs

"I think **a simple rule of business is,** if you do the things that are **easier first**, then you can actually make a lot of progress."

Quotes from the Greatest Entrepreneurs

"**Facebook was not originally created to be a company.** It was built to accomplish a social mission—to make the world **more open and connected.**"

Mark Zuckerberg

"We don't build services to make money; **we make money to build better services.**"

WRITE A BIOGRAPHY

Life Story

A person's life story can be the subject of a book. This kind of book is called a **biography**. Biographies often describe the lives of people who have achieved great success. These people may be alive today, or they may have lived many years ago. Reading a biography can help you learn more about a great person.

Help and Obstacles

- Did this individual have a positive attitude?
- Did this person have a **mentor**?
- Did this person face any hardships?
- If so, how were the hardships overcome?

Biography Brainstorming

Childhood

- Where and when was this person born?
- Describe his or her parents, siblings, and friends.
- Did this person grow up in unusual circumstances?

Success in the Workforce

- What records does this person hold?
- What has he or she achieved?
- How does he or she measure professional success?

Get the Facts

Use this book, and research in the library and on the internet, to find out more about your favorite **entrepreneur**. Learn as much about this person as you can. Where did his or her first big idea come from? What are his or her strategies for success? Has he or she set any records? Also, be sure to write down key events in the person's life. What was his or her childhood like? What has he or she accomplished? Is there anything else that makes this person special or unusual?

Accomplishments
- What is this person's life's work?
- Has he or she received awards or recognition for accomplishments?
- How have this person's accomplishments served others?

Your Opinion
- What did you learn from the books you read in your research?
- Would you suggest these books to others?
- Was anything missing from these books?

Creating a Biography
Brainstorming can be a useful research tool. Read the questions listed in each category. Answer these questions in your notebook. Your answers will help you write a biography.

Work and Preparation
- What was this person's education?
- What was his or her work experience?
- How does this person work? What is the process he or she uses?

Adulthood
- Does he or she have a family?
- What roles have prepared him or her for a career as an entrepreneur?
- How have his or her relationships influenced his or her success?

BY THE NUMBERS

Many **milestones** mark the path of a successful entrepreneur. Each achievement offers a glimpse into the life and career of Mark Zuckerberg. Consider these fascinating facts to gain a better understanding of the man behind the quotes.

23
The age Zuckerberg became the
world's youngest
self-made millionaire.

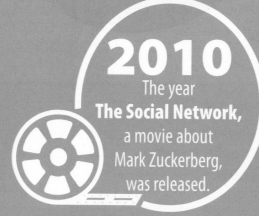

2010
The year
The Social Network,
a movie about
Mark Zuckerberg,
was released.

8,348
The number of people
employed at Facebook.

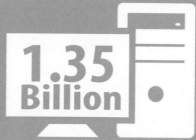

1.35 Billion
The number of people
who use Facebook
every month.

$100 Million
The amount Zuckerberg
pledged to donate to the
Newark, New Jersey
school system.

KEY WORDS

biography: an account of a person's life, written by another person

entrepreneur: someone who starts a business and assumes any potential risks associated with it

mentor: a trusted and experienced advisor

milestones: significant events or achievements

social media: online services that allow people to communicate

software: the programing needed to operate computers

INDEX

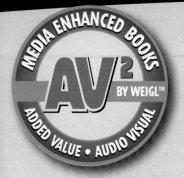

Log on to www.av2books.com

AV² by Weigl brings you media enhanced books that support active learning. Go to www.av2books.com, and enter the special code found on page 2 of this book. You will gain access to enriched and enhanced content that supplements and complements this book. Content includes video, audio, weblinks, quizzes, a slide show, and activities.

AV² Online Navigation

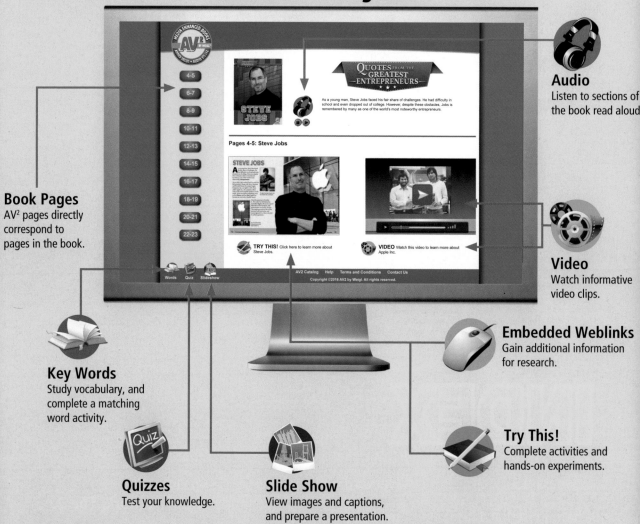

Audio
Listen to sections of the book read aloud

Book Pages
AV² pages directly correspond to pages in the book.

Video
Watch informative video clips.

Key Words
Study vocabulary, and complete a matching word activity.

Embedded Weblinks
Gain additional information for research.

Quizzes
Test your knowledge.

Slide Show
View images and captions, and prepare a presentation.

Try This!
Complete activities and hands-on experiments.

AV² was built to bridge the gap between print and digital. We encourage you to tell us what you like and what you want to see in the future.

Sign up to be an AV² Ambassador at www.av2books.com/ambassador.

Due to the dynamic nature of the Internet, some of the URLs and activities provided as part of AV² by Weigl may have changed or ceased to exist. AV² by Weigl accepts no responsibility for any such changes. All media enhanced books are regularly monitored to update addresses and sites in a timely manner. Contact AV² by Weigl at 1-866-649-3445 or av2books@weigl.com with any questions, comments, or feedback.